Write Right

by Bronwyn Miller
illustrated by Liz Callen

Practice Decodable 69

McGraw Hill Education

Bothell, WA • Chicago, IL • Columbus, OH • New York, NY

MHEonline.com

Send all inquiries to:
McGraw-Hill Education
8787 Orion Place
Columbus, OH 43240

ISBN: 978-0-02-130427-1
MHID: 0-02-130427-0

Printed in the United States of America.

7 8 9 CTM 23

On the first day of class, Dennis looked at all the kids writing.

The kids used their right hands. Did he write the wrong way?

Dennis tried writing with his right hand. He wrinkled his face. His wrist hurt.

Miss Wren looked at Dennis.

"What's wrong?" she asked. Then she saw Dennis writing with his right hand.

"Dennis, write this way," she said.

"But no one writes with their left hand," said Dennis.

"Some teachers do," said Miss Wren.
Then she wrote with her left hand.
Dennis was happy now!